I0172921

Isaiah
A Book of Comfort

Joanne Ellison

JOANNE ELLISON

JOANNE ELLISON

CONTENTS

JOANNE ELLISON

JOANNE ELLISON

LESSON FORMAT

The courses offered through Drawing Near to God are developed to bring out life application of the scriptures. Using books of the Bible as the backdrop for themes in Scripture, you will travel back and forth through the Old and New Testaments to help knit the whole story of the Gospel together.

In each lesson, there is a scripture for meditation, a main theme, and three topics in which the theme will be expanded. I suggest that you read the Key Passage in each section and personalize it by asking the question, "How does this apply to my life?" Writing down thoughts for reflection will help you learn the key points of the study.

A Key Box is included in each section with comments that provide insight related to the topic. This is followed by scriptural references and a series of questions to reinforce the contents of the scripture. There is ample space to write your insights and a life application section at the end of each lesson to reinforce what you have learned. Each section ends with prayer.

1 THE HUMAN CONDITION

The human condition of sin has existed since the Garden of Eden when Adam and Eve rebelled against God and ate from the Tree of Knowledge of Good and Evil which the Lord had forbidden them to do. Temptation will always be with us, but it doesn't become sin until we act on it. Throughout Isaiah, we see God's people give in to the temptation to forsake the Lord, but whenever they turned back to Him, He restored them. Jesus Christ has restored the human condition by offering us the gift of forgiveness through His death on the cross. We are a people of hope restored by a God who is full of mercy.

Meditation
....they have forsaken the Lord; they have spurned the Holy One of Israel and turned their backs on Him. Isaiah 1:4

Main Theme

As you read the Main Theme, underline words or thoughts most meaningful to you.

In the time of Isaiah, the Israelites, God's chosen people, once again turned from God. In the opening chapters of Isaiah, God admonishes His people through the prophet Isaiah concerning their corruption and rebellion. We, too, repeatedly like sheep go astray, each of us turning to our own way and forsaking God. (Isaiah 53:6) God continually calls us back in His mercy because He loves us. Although the human condition of sin persists throughout the generations, God's mercy and unfailing love persist in bringing us back to Him.

Lesson Focus
Read Isaiah 1 through 5.

I. Missing the Mark

- Key Passage: Isaiah 53:6

> The Greek word for sin is "hamartia" which translates "to miss the mark." When we sin, we miss the mark of obtaining God's best for our lives. My son loves to bow hunt for deer. In order to shoot the deer, he must line up the animal in the "sight" of the bow or else he will miss the target completely. When we do not keep God "in sight," we fall prey to sin. We must align ourselves with God's Word in order to stay on target and hit the mark and assure ourselves of being in God's will.

What stood out to you as you read the Key Box?

_____

_____

_____

Genesis 4:1-12

- Why didn't God accept Cain's offering with favor?

_____

_____

Genesis 4:7

- Applying the story of Cain and Abel, what causes sin to "crouch at the door" of our lives?

_____

_____

Exodus 32:1-26

- What happened when Moses was "so long in coming down" from meeting with God on the mountain?

_____

_____

- What happened to the people when they chose to worship other gods, and how should we apply this lesson to our lives today?

_____

_____

Numbers 32:23, Psalm 51:4

- When we sin, who are we sinning against?

_____

_____

Romans 7:14-20

- Why does Paul say that he is a slave to sin?

_____

_____

- What area of your life do you fall prey to "missing the mark"?

_____

_____

<u>John 1:29 and I John 2:1-2</u>

- Who takes away our sins and advocates for us?

_____

_____

Seeking God is the first step towards turning from our sins. J. Alec Motyer in his commentary on Isaiah states that "seeking God is not looking for Him as though He were lost, but showing a determination to be with Him where He may be found." The Israelites had turned from God; God had not turned from them.

II. Humbled and Renewed

- Key Passage: Romans 7:23-24

Isaiah describes the condition of Israel as a nation filled with guilt. The human condition of our fallen nature perpetuates a cycle of sin where, like Paul, we do what we don't want to do. (Romans 7:14-20) The Israelites had forsaken the Lord and their condition was seemingly hopeless. Isaiah 1:27 gives us hope that the penitent will be redeemed. We, too, sometimes feel hopeless and burdened with guilt, but Jesus Christ offers us a solution to our condition through His offer of forgiveness by His shed blood on the cross. (Hebrews 9:22)

What stood out to you as you read the Key Box?

_____

_____

_____

Isaiah 2:6-11

- What sins had the people of Jerusalem committed?

_____

_____

Isaiah 9:13-18

- What had the people of Israel neglected to do, and whom does the Lord hold responsible for misguiding the people?

_____

_____

Isaiah 1:27

- What hope does God give the people for restoration, and what is the condition for restoration?

_____

_____

Jeremiah 15:18-19-21

- What further hope does this offer to those who turn from their sinful ways and turn back to God?

_____

_____

Isaiah 3:14 - 4:4-6

- How does the Lord redeem the women described in Isaiah 3:16, and how does knowing that God is willing to redeem help us in our walk with Him?

_____

_____

Isaiah 57:14-18, Psalm 51:16-17

- What condition of the heart is the Lord looking for in order to comfort, revive, and redeem?

_____

_____

Ephesians 1:3-8

- According to this, how are our sins redeemed?

_____

_____

- What gives you the assurance that Christ has forgiven and redeemed your sins?

_____

_____

The opening chapters of Isaiah take us on a journey of highs and lows as we read about a people who have forsaken God, and yet, we see that God offers redemption to those who turn to Him. As a people today who also forsake God, it is great to have the assurance that God relentlessly pursues us even to the extent of sending His only Son to die for our sins!!

III. Sincere Worship

- Key Passage: Hebrews 10:22

Burnt offerings were offered every morning and every evening for all of Israel. (Exodus 29:38-42) The Hebrew name "minhah" for burnt offerings means "gift" or "sacrifice." The Israelites worshipped God through sacrificing animals. God speaks through Isaiah telling the Israelites that their burnt offerings are meaningless. (Isaiah 1:11-13) God looks at our hearts to see if our attitude of worship is sincere or if we are simply going through the motions. I pray that during our study of Isaiah, God will pierce our hearts and our worship will grow in sincerity and purity.

What stood out to you as you read the Key Box?

_____

_____

_____

Psalm 95, Psalm 100 and Isaiah 12:1-6

- Describe in your own words how the Psalms listed above and Isaiah encourage you to worship God.

_____

_____

- What are several of the keys to worshipping God that are set forth in Psalm 100?

_____

_____

John 4:7-24

- While speaking to the woman at the well, what kind of worshippers did Jesus say the Father was seeking?

  _____

  _____

- How do you think that our worship today can become meaningless?

  _____

  _____

Romans 12:1-2

- How does Paul describe our spiritual act of worship?

  _____

  _____

Hebrews 10:1-10

- According to this, why were the animal sacrifices not able to perfect worship?

  _____

  _____

- Who replaced the Old Testament sacrifices?

  _____

  _____

- How does knowing this encourage us to receive Jesus as our sacrifice for our sins and to worship God with a new heart?

  _____

  _____

LIFE APPLICATION

- ✟ Acknowledge your human condition of sin.

- ✟ Receive the gift of Christ into your life for the forgiveness of your sins.

- ✟ Begin to worship Him with a new heart.

- ✟ Personalize and journal the verses in Psalm 100 that have the most meaning for you.

- ✟ Reflect on your sphere of influence and ask the Lord to help you to be "salt and light" to them, and to redeem any situation where you may have misguided others in thought, word, or deed. (Isaiah 3:14 and Isaiah 9:15-16)

PRAYER

Dear Lord, grant me forgiveness for all my sins, true repentance, a new life, and the grace and comfort of your Holy Spirit.

Paraphrased
Disciplines for the Inner Life
Rob Benson, Michael W. Benson

2 THE MAJESTY OF GOD

This week we focus on understanding the Majesty of God as well as the concept of God drawing near to us through His Son, Jesus Christ. Try to relate to King Ahaz as Isaiah encourages him to stand firm in his faith. When we stand firm in our faith, the light of Christ pierces even our darkest of times offering us hope and contentment in our daily lives.

Meditation
...the Lord Himself will give you a sign: The virgin will be with child and will give birth to a son, and will call him Immanuel. Isaiah 7:14

Main Theme

As you read the Main Theme, underline words or thoughts most meaningful to you.

The book of Isaiah foretells the birth of Christ and His dwelling among us. The name "Immanuel" means "God with us." Throughout Isaiah, we see God reaching out to humanity with both His love and His judgment. He created us in His image, and His plan was for people to be in relationship with Him. After the fall of Adam and Eve, God's plan of restoring mankind back into relationship with Him was set in motion. His only Son, Jesus Christ, was sent to bring us back to the Father, and He fulfilled this purpose on the cross. In this section of our study, we read the prophecy that Christ, "Immanuel," has come to us and has brought His eternal light into our lives so that we might once again draw near to God.

Lesson Focus
Read Isaiah 6 through 9

I. The Majesty of God

- Key Passage: Psalm 8:1-9

When the prophet Isaiah had a vision of God seated on His throne, he was undone. God's majesty and His holiness caused him to cry out, "Woe to me! I am ruined! For I am a man of unclean lips, and I live among a people of unclean lips, and my eyes have seen the King, the Lord Almighty." (Isaiah 6:5) Isaiah recognized that he could not stand before the God of all Ages, before His majesty and holiness, and not have his sins exposed. As I read through the passage in Isaiah 6:1-5 in preparation for this lesson, I closed my eyes and imagined the Lord, high and lifted up, and my standing before Him with my life exposed. I, too, cried out with Isaiah, "Woe to me! I am ruined!" Then I remembered Immanuel, God with us, the One whom God sent to restore me and to enable me to be in His presence. With great relief and awe, I thanked God for making a way for me to draw near to Him through His Son Jesus Christ.

What stood out to you as you read the Key Box?

_____

_____

_____

Exodus 15:6-13

- How is God described here, and what did He accomplish with His majestic power?

_____

_____

Isaiah 6:1-10

- Write in your own words the description of the majesty and holiness of God.

_____

_____

Isaiah 2:6-11

- Why did the people have to hide from the majesty of God?

_____

_____

Hebrews 1:1-3

- What are the shared relationship attributes between God and the Son in this passage?

_____

_____

Exodus 33:12-23

- According to this passage, how is the glory of God described?

_____

_____

When we catch but a glimpse of God's glory, His holiness, and His majesty, we are forever changed. Thank God for His transforming Presence in our lives!

II. Standing Firm in Faith

- Key Passage: Isaiah 7:9b

> We read in Isaiah 7:1-9 the account of Ahaz, King of Judah, whose "heart was shaken" as his enemies aligned themselves against him. Isaiah was sent by God to encourage Ahaz to stay calm and not to be afraid. He explains to Ahaz how events will turn out and reminds him that he must stand firm in his faith in God. Just as King Jehoshaphat was reminded in II Chronicles 20:15 that the battle belongs to the Lord, so King Ahaz must remember that when he puts his trust in God, it is God who will fight the battle. We, too, must often be reminded that although we face the battles of life, God will go before us and fight our battles as we stand firm in our faith.

What stood out to you as you read the Key Box?

_____

_____

_____

<u>Isaiah 26:1-5</u>

- What is the distinguishing mark of a nation where God permits the gates of freedom to be opened?

_____

_____

- What is the key factor in keeping our minds steadfast?

_____

_____

- In what area of your life is your mind not steadfast and your trust in God wavering?

_____

_____

II Chronicles 20:15-20

- What did King Jehoshaphat tell the people to do in order to be upheld and win the battle?

_____

_____

Ephesians 6:10-18

- According to this passage, who attacks our faith?

_____

_____

- What must we do to protect our faith?

_____

_____

Luke 22:31-32

- What does Jesus say He will do for Simon (Peter) when Satan attacks Peter's faith?

_____

_____

Romans 4:18-21

- What was Abraham's defense against his faith weakening?

_____

_____

III. The Dawning Light

- Key Passage: Isaiah 9:2

> Isaiah 9 opens with a description of the Messiah, God Immanuel, who will come to dwell with the people. The people of Isaiah's time walked in darkness, just as many people today walk in darkness. Jesus Christ, the Messiah, came and brought a "great light" into the world. This great light provides a hope for all mankind. The prophecies of Isaiah describe and point to the light of hope for all those in darkness. Do you know the One who lights the way out of darkness?

What stood out to you as you read the Key Box?

_____

_____

_____

Psalm 18:28-29

- According to King David, who keeps our lamps burning, i.e. our spiritual lives flourishing?

_____

_____

<u>Psalm 27:1-3</u>

- Why is David fearless when his foes attack him?

_____

_____

- When you are under attack, how can Christ's light dispel the darkness and give you strength?

_____

_____

<u>Matthew 4:12-17, Isaiah 9:1-2 and Isaiah 42:6-7, 16</u>

- How does Matthew relate to the prophecies in the Isaiah verses listed above?

_____

_____

God is at work in us as we go about our daily routine of life. God is with us as we seek His help in times of struggle. God is with us as we seek His direction: Immanuel, God with us, Christ in us, our Hope that brings us light when we walk in darkness!

LIFE APPLICATION

- ✛ Pray that the eyes of your heart will be opened to see the majesty of God. (Ephesians 1:17-20)

- ✛ Take a moment and evaluate your life of faith.

- ✛ Stand firm in your faith.

- ✛ Invite Christ's light to reveal any darkness in your life. (Psalm 139:23-24)

- ✛ Repent and turn from anything He shows you so that you can walk in His light..

- ✛ Journal about areas where you sense that your faith is weak and ask the Lord to renew your faith and trust in Him so that you can have success in the battles you face.

PRAYER

Dear Lord, I pray that You will open the eyes of my heart through the glorious light of Christ, in order that I might see Your majesty, know the hope to which I have been called, and walk in Your resurrection power.

Personalized from Ephesians 1:17-20

3 DRAWING FROM THE SPRINGS OF SALVATION

Throughout the Old Testament, the Scriptures point to Jesus as the "well of salvation". This week's study will focus on the Messianic passage pointing to Jesus in Isaiah 11 as the "shoot from the stump of Jesse". (Jesse was the father of King David) Throughout Scripture, there are many prophecies that point to Jesus. We will also be looking at the importance of Godly leadership and the significance of being part of the "faithful remnant" requiring us to draw from the springs of salvation through Jesus Christ.

Meditation
....whoever drinks the water I give him will never thirst. Indeed, the water I give him will become in him a spring of water welling up to eternal life. John 4:14

Main Theme

As you read the Main Theme, underline words or thoughts most meaningful to you.

The Hebrew word for salvation "yeshua" (yesh-oo-aw) means deliverance, aid, victory, and prosperity. It is derived from the root word "yaw-shah" meaning to be open, wide, or free. Isaiah 12:2-3 describes the songs of praise that the Israelites would one day sing about their deliverance from the Assyrians. They would be restored and they would drink from God's salvation or "well of deliverance." This text also looks towards the Eternal Well, Jesus Christ (Yeshua), who would bring ultimate salvation, enabling people everywhere to drink from His eternal well.

Lesson Focus
Read Isaiah 10 through 12.

I. Salvation In Jesus

- Key Passage: Acts 2:21

> In Isaiah 7:13-14, Isaiah prophesies to King Ahaz, "Hear now, you house of David!....The Lord will give you a sign: The virgin will be with child and will give birth to a son, and will call Him Immanuel." 750 years later God carried out His promise. Jesus said that He was the fulfillment of the prophecies concerning the Messiah, the One who would ultimately bring freedom to the captives. During the Advent season, we are reminded that Jesus came to earth to save us and everyone who calls on His name. (Acts 2:21)

What stood out to you as you read the Key Box?

_____

_____

_____

Isaiah 11:1-10

- According to the prophecy in Isaiah 11:1, from whom did a "shoot" appear?

_____

_____

I Samuel 16:1-12

- Which of Jesse's sons was anointed to be King of Israel?

_____

_____

Isaiah 9:1-7

- In the Messianic passage describing the coming of Jesus, on whose throne will Christ reign?

_____

_____

Isaiah 61:1 and Luke 4:14-19

- What did Jesus come to do according to these passages?

_____

_____

Isaiah 11:1-3

- Like King David, who would empower the Messiah?

_____

_____

- What holds you captive and how is Jesus working in your life to bring about your deliverance and freedom?

_____

_____

Isaiah 12:3 and John 4:10-14

- What does it mean to "draw water from the springs of salvation"?

_____

_____

The Assyrians almost completely destroyed Judah, but it was the Babylonian exile that brought the kingdom of Judah to an end in 586 BC. The Messiah, Jesus Christ, grew as a shoot from the stump of David's dynasty and His kingdom will have no end. (Isaiah 9:7) Is His kingdom ruling and reigning in your heart?

II. The Head and the Tail

- Key Passage: Ezekiel 34:2

Throughout the book of Isaiah, the prophet condemns the leadership of the people. As Christian leaders, we are called to set an example for the ungodly. The elders of Israel (the head) and the prophets (the tail) were misguiding the people. (Isaiah 9:15-16) In Isaiah 10, we read that the lawmakers issued "oppressive decrees" and withheld justice. It is our responsibility to be leaders in our society today, exemplifying the character of Christ.

What stood out to you as you read the Key Box?

_____

_____

_____

Isaiah 9:14-16

- Who is referred to by the "tail" and the "head"?

_____

_____

- How can we as Christian leaders effectively be the "head" and the "tail"?

_____

_____

Ezekiel 34:1-5, Isaiah 40:10-11

- Describe how the shepherd leaders in Ezekiel cared for their sheep, and compare our leaders today.

  _____

  _____

- Who are you leading, and what can you do to improve in your leadership skills?

  _____

  _____

Think about what it is like to travel with young children. Before take-off, the pre-flight instructions include what to do if there is oxygen loss and how you are to assist children. First you secure the oxygen mask over your nose, and then you help your child by putting on his/her oxygen mask. As Christian leaders, we can only be effective in leading others by first insuring that we are "breathing in the Holy Spirit." Isaiah 11 describes what the oxygen of the Holy Spirit is like: wisdom, understanding, counsel, power, and fear of the Lord. When we walk with a "full tank," we can help others to draw from the springs of salvation as well.

III. A Faithful Remnant

- Key Passage: Acts 3:19

The son of Isaiah was called Shear-jashub which means "a remnant shall return." The House of David had to eat curds and honey, the food of poverty, because the invading Assyrian army decimated the countryside. They learned, however, through this difficult time to "refuse evil and choose good." Shear-jashub represents the return of the remnant back to the Lord and thus back to a time of prosperity. The Lord has promised throughout the ages that if we turn from evil and seek to obey the Lord, He will bring us back from captivity. There has always been a faithful remnant who have continued to turn to the Lord. I pray that we will all be a part of the faithful.

What stood out to you as you read the Key Box?

_____

_____

_____

Romans 11:1-12

- Why did God not reject His people?

_____

_____

- What does the passage mean to you personally, "and if by grace, then it is no longer by works"?

_____

_____

Isaiah 10:20-22

- What will be the distinguishing mark of the remnant?

_____

_____

- Where are you not relying on the Lord, and are you able to describe the destruction that this brings into your "spiritual land"?

_____

_____

Isaiah 28:5-6

- What does this passage say will be the reward of the remnant?

_____

_____

Jesus looked out over Jerusalem and said that He longed to gather the chicks like a mother hen. He longed to draw the Jews to Himself, the well of salvation, a place of security, peace, and deliverance. The people of Jerusalem rejected Jesus just as the people of Isaiah's time had rejected God. Let us be a people who are willing to go forth "with joy, drawing from the well of salvation" as a part of the faithful remnant. (Isaiah 12:3)

LIFE APPLICATION

✚ Seek the Lord who brings salvation.

✚ Pray for deliverance.

✚ Daily draw from God's eternal spring of salvation.

PRAYER

O LORD, be gracious to me; I long for you. Be my strength every morning, my salvation in time of distress.

Isaiah 33:2

4 THE CONFLICT WITHIN

Many people struggle with conflicts in their lives both internally and externally. Hopefully you are beginning to open your heart and allow the Holy Spirit to help you lay aside anything that obstructs your relationship with the Lord. Often our sense of self sufficiency, pride, and reliance on the world to offer us solutions falls short. Isaiah, the prophet not only spoke to the Israelites who were struggling with these things, he was speaking to us as well through the sacred scriptures. Simply put, we need to be dependent on God to lead and direct our lives. A door has been opened for freedom, peace and hope through His Son Jesus Christ. We are blessed to live on this side of the cross!

Meditation
Oh, the raging of many nations- they rage like the raging sea! Oh, the uproar of the peoples- they roar like the roaring of great waters! Isaiah 17:12

Main Theme
As you read the Main Theme, underline words or thoughts most meaningful to you.

This section of Isaiah addresses the question: Why is peace on earth still a distant objective? The prophecies contained in these chapters concern the great world powers that surrounded Israel in that day. These nations not only represent events in history, they also represent forces at work on earth throughout the ages. The experience of these nations represents our own personal struggles as well. Why don't the nations live in peace? Why does peace evade us as individuals? The forces at work in the nations in the time of Isaiah were pride, materialism, deception, and self-sufficiency. When these forces are at work in our individual lives, it becomes apparent that the

"Prince of Peace" has been removed from the throne of our lives and peace inevitably will be disrupted in our lives.

Lesson Focus
Read Isaiah 13 through 29.

I. The Self-Sufficiency of Babylon

- Key Passage: Isaiah 17:10-12

The nations that raged in the time of Isaiah were filled with turmoil. The city of Babylon is seen throughout both the Old and New Testaments as a city plagued with pride and self-sufficiency. Babylon symbolizes the world powers arrayed against God's kingdom. Throughout the ages, we see other cities and nations plagued by self-sufficiency, finding no need for God. We, too, as individuals, fall prey to being self-sufficient and tend to forget God, our Savior, forgetting our Rock, our Fortress. (Isaiah 17:10)

What stood out to you as you read the Key Box?

_____

_____

_____

Genesis 11:1-8

- What was the tower of Babel, and what happened to it and the people

_____

_____

- What motivated the people to build the tower, and why do you think that God scattered the people because they built it?

_____

_____

Luke 1:51

- According to Mary's song in Luke, why did God scatter the people? Can you recall a time when you were walking in pride and you felt "scattered" or removed from Him?

_____

_____

Ephesians 6:12

- According to Ephesians, who is behind the "turmoil" within us?

_____

_____

Isaiah 13-14

- Why did Babylon fall? How does this apply to our nation and to you individually?

_____

_____

Revelation 18:1-3

- What is at the root of Babylon's fall?

_____

_____

When we catch but a glimpse of God's glory, His holiness, and His majesty, we are forever changed. Thank God for His transforming Presence in our lives!!

II. The Materialism of Tyre

- Key Passage: Matthew 6:19-21.

> Tyre was the main seaport along the Phoenician coast. Part of the city was built on two rocky islands one-half mile from shore. The ships of Tarshish were laden with goods and wealth of the nations. Nebuchadnezer captured the mainland city (572 BC), but the island was not taken until Alexander the Great destroyed it in 332 BC. The city of Tyre represents a nation that was full of pride in its wealth. She had become the marketplace for the nations. (Isaiah 23:3) The Lord brought Tyre low and humbled "the pride of her glory." We see today in many nations the pride of wealth, particularly in the United States. As individuals, we, too, can easily be caught up in the "tyranny of Tyre."

What stood out to you as you read the Key Box?

_____

_____

_____

Ezekiel 28:1-2

- What did Ezekiel say to the King of Tyre that exposes the root of the tyranny of Tyre?

_____

_____

Ezekiel 28: 11-17

- How did the King of Tyre fall from an anointed place in God's kingdom to a place where he was driven out of God's presence?

_____

_____

Joel 3:1-6

- What did the cities of Tyre and Sidon do that brought God's judgment on them?

_____

_____

Matthew 11:20-22

- How did Jesus compare Tyre and Sidon to Korazin and Bethsaida, and what was the redeeming quality that Tyre and Sidon possessed?

_____

_____

I Kings 5:1-9

- How did the King of Tyre in this passage exemplify how wealth can be used for God's purposes?

_____

_____

Tyre was eventually besieged by the Babylonians in 586 BC and captured by the Greeks in 332 BC. God judges materialism in nations and in our personal lives. The Lord's unfailing love, however, draws us to repentance when we see the tyranny of materialism. There is no silver, gold, or diamond that is more precious than He is.

III. The Pride of Moab

- Key Passage: I Peter 5:5

> The self-sufficiency of Babylon, the materialism of Tyre, and the independence of Moab all had pride as the root of their sins. Isaiah describes the people of Moab as "high fortified walls." (Isaiah 25:12) The pride of these nations caused their destruction. Pride is the insidious enemy within us that tries to destroy humility. Yet God tells us in His Word that He dwells with the humble and contrite of heart. (Isaiah 57:15) We, too, must be willing to allow the Lord to bring down the strongholds of pride in our lives so that the humble King of Kings can dwell in us.

What stood out to you as you read the Key Box?

_____

_____

_____

Genesis 19:30-37

- According to the passage in Genesis, who was Moab and how was he conceived?

_____

_____

I Samuel 14:47 and II Chronicles 20:1-12

- In these Scripture passages, who were the enemies of the Israelites?

_____

_____

Isaiah 25:10-12

- What does God promise?

_____

_____

- How does pride destroy the purposes of God in your life, and what are the steps according to today's lesson that you must take to bring down the "high fortified wall" of pride?

_____

_____

Galatians 5:16-24

- Contrast the "fruit of the Spirit" with the "sins of the flesh."

_____

_____

LIFE APPLICATION

✠ Pray that the Lord will release in you the desire to use your resources for God's purposes and to soften your heart if you struggle in this area of your life.

✠ Pray that the Lord reveal any areas of pride, self-sufficiency, or materialism in your life.

✠ Turn to the Lord in repentance.

PRAYER

Search me, O God, and know my heart; test me and know my anxious thoughts. See if there is any offensive way in me, and lead me in the way everlasting.

Psalm 139: 23-24

5 REST FOR OUR SOULS

We live at such a fast pace today and rest for our soul appears to be impossible. This week's discussion will examine the "ways of Egypt" in our lives; those things that keep us in bondage, robbing us of peace. Remember the Israelites' journey out of Egypt after 400 years of slavery as they sought to get to the Promised Land. We too must leave our place of bondage in order to find rest. It may be for some members a "should", "ought", or "have to" mentality has been self-imposed in their life. For example, we may take on something out of guilt rather than out of a sense of a call from God. In section II we learn that God will direct our path to freedom and rest and in section III, we will find rest when we are rightly aligned with God.

Meditation

In repentance and rest is your salvation; in quietness and trust is your strength. Isaiah 30:15

Main Theme

As you read the Main Theme, underline words or thoughts most meaningful to you.

For many of us, rest seems to be an elusive concept. Both physical and spiritual rest seem to be under attack in the 21st century today. If you simply look in the stores, you will find creams claiming to reduce stress, fragrances to alleviate tension, and music with titles to suggest relaxation. We indeed live in a fast-paced world that demands our time and energy and finds us searching for ways to find rest. Isaiah's recipe for national security, according to theologian Alec Motyer, is, "First there should be repentance and returning to the Lord. This would bring rest. Then there is quietness, the absence of frenzy and restless activity, which evidences a true trust. This brings strength for life's battles and challenges." So it is with us when we turn back to the Lord and choose to trust Him, to cease from "frenzy and restless activity," He gives us strength amidst a restless and fast-paced world.

Lesson Focus
Read Isaiah 30 through 34

    I.   Going Down to Egypt

- Key Passage: Proverbs 3:5

    "Woe to those who go down to Egypt for help, who rely on horses, who trust in the multitude of their chariots and in the great strength of their horseman, but do not look to the Holy One of Israel, or seek help from the Lord."(Isaiah 31:1) These are the words penned by the prophet Isaiah describing Israel's reliance on Egypt who represented wealth, false security, prosperity, and human wisdom. It is so interesting to me that in former years the Israelites had served as slaves to the Egyptians who were hard taskmasters. Moses led the people out of Egypt and ultimately they rested in the Promised Land. How quickly the Israelites forgot their life of slavery as they remembered the "benefits" of Egypt. We, too, can easily become enslaved by forgetting the Lord and relying on "things" or on "human wisdom" to bring us peace and understanding when our only true peace comes through trusting in the Lord.

What stood out to you as you read the Key Box?

_____

_____

_____

Genesis 26:1-6 and Isaiah 30:1-9

- Why do you think that Isaac would have wanted to go down to Egypt?

_____

_____

- Using these Scriptures, what were the reasons that God appeared to Isaac telling him not to go to Egypt?

_____

_____

Exodus 3:7-12

- Why did the Lord tell Moses that He was sending him to lead the Israelites out of Egypt?

_____

_____

- What is your "Egypt" that enslaves you, leaving you feeling restless and robbing you of peace?

_____

_____

Isaiah 26:3-4 and Isaiah 30:15

- What goes hand in hand with your being at "rest"?

_____

_____

- In order to repent and turn back to God, what must you do?

_____

_____

God in His infinite mercy and love sent us Jesus Christ to be "a precious Cornerstone for a sure foundation." (Isaiah 28:16) We are promised that when we put our trust in Him, Egypt cannot have a hold on us.

II. Redirecting Our Faith

- Key Passage: Isaiah 30:18

> The Lord longs to be gracious and is full of compassion when He hears our cry for help. It gives me great comfort to know that He longs for me to cry out to Him so He can redirect my path. Isaiah 28 and 29 describe the six "woes" that we all fall into that take us off course. The first "woe" is written to Ephraim, the northern kingdom of Israel. History tells us that the people of Samaria, the capital city, were given over to the love of fleshly pleasures. With each of the warnings, Isaiah gives a way of escape. The other "woes" were meaningless, empty, religious rituals, hidden evil deeds, rebellion, arrogance, and misplaced confidence. When we fall into any of these traps, Isaiah gives us comfort by saying, "Whether you turn to the right or to the left, your ears will hear a voice behind you saying this is the way; walk in it." (Isaiah 30:21)

What stood out to you as you read the Key Box?

_____

_____

_____

Proverbs 3:1-6 & Isaiah 2:3

- What enables us to walk on a godly path?

_____

_____

Isaiah 30:19-21

- Describe how you hear God's saying, "This is the way; walk in it."

_____

_____

Because God's ways are not our ways, if He redirects our path it might seem foreign or uncertain to us. However, we can be sure that if we put our trust in Him, we will find rest for our souls.

III. Aligning with God

• Key Passage: Psalm 23:3

Once the Lord shows us that we are on the wrong path, it is essential that we agree with His plan and follow His way. Isaiah warned the people that they were obstinate because they carried out their own plans rather than the plans of the Lord, forming an alliance, but not by His Spirit. (Isaiah 30:1) They consulted with the Pharaoh of Egypt, aligning themselves with ungodly advice (human wisdom and reasoning) and sought protection from the Pharaoh. Their sin, according to Isaiah, was like a "high wall, cracked and bulging, collapsing suddenly." (Isaiah 30:13). We, too, have our "high walls" built on human reasoning and unholy alliances. The Lord is calling us to come into agreement with His Word. The rebellious people in Isaiah's day told the prophets to tell them only pleasant things and to stop confronting them with the Holy One of Israel. (Isaiah 30:10) In our nation today and in our personal lives we can hear the cry of many saying, "Don't tell me any more bad news about God's judgment; don't confront me with the truth of Scripture." I pray that the Lord will help us to be willing to align ourselves with His truth. May we also be willing to confront the places of complacency in our own spiritual lives, and be willing to bring His light to a confused and broken world.

What stood out to you as you read the Key Box?

_____

_____

_____

Isaiah 5:20

- How does coming out of alignment with God's Word and calling "evil good and good evil" give the enemy an opportunity to wreak havoc in our lives?

_____

_____

Isaiah 1:18-19

- If you are presently not in alignment with God in any area of your life, how can you personally apply this scripture?

_____

_____

Isaiah 32:1-2

- What is the promise that is given to God's redeemed when they return to Him?

_____

_____

- How does aligning ourselves with God allow us to be a refuge of living water to others?

_____

_____

God longs for us to follow His path, to agree with His precepts, and to be a refuge for others in the storms of life. Are you willing to follow His way and allow Him to direct your path so that you can find rest for your souls and offer rest to others in need?

LIFE APPLICATION

- ☥ Pray that the Lord will reveal any area in your life where you are not at peace and surrender that area to Him.

- ☥ Ask the Lord to show you in what ways He needs to direct your path.

- ☥ Pray for the grace to follow His path and not your own.

- ☥ In your journal, write down what you believe the Lord is telling you.

- ☥ Seek ways to help others find rest in salvation, quietness, and trust in God's strength. (Isaiah 30:15)

PRAYER

Show me your ways, O LORD, teach me your paths; guide me in Your truth and teach me, for You are God, my Savior, and my hope is in You all day long.

Psalm 25:4-5

6 GOD'S STRENGTH TO DELIVER

This week we will see God's hand delivering us from the assault of the enemy. Focus on the ways in which you are under attack and that it is God's strength that will sustain and deliver us. A primary trap that we fall into is depending on our own strength to deliver us. Focus on Gideon this week (Judges 6) and how he quickly learned to depend on God. In section II focus on God's peace verses false peace. False peace, simply put, is depending on anything other than God. Another trap we fall into is looking at our circumstances rather than at the Lord. Take time to review the story of Peter (Matthew 14:22-31) and how his initial trust enabled him to walk on water however when he looked down at the rough water (ie-circumstances) he began to sink.

Meditation

Strengthen the feeble hands, steady the knees that give way; say to those with fearful hearts, "Be strong, do not fear; your God will come, He will come with vengeance; with divine retribution He will come to save you." Isaiah 35:3-4

Main Theme

As you read the Main Theme, underline words or thoughts most meaningful to you.

Let us remember as we study the book of Isaiah the words of the Apostle Paul, "These things happened to them as an example and were written down as warnings for us, on whom the fulfillment of the ages has come."(I Corinthians 10:11) The judgments set against the people of Israel depict things that are true of us. Babylon, Tyre, Assyria, and Egypt appear all the way through the Scriptures and they illustrated the world in its varied attack upon believers. In Isaiah 35-37, we see the attack of Assyria against God's people. Assyria is a picture of the violence and cruelty of the world, and these chapters give an account of the fading of Assyria from the Biblical scene and the rise of the nation Babylon. Assyria was the main threat to Israel in the first half of this book, while in the second half Babylon becomes Israel's prime enemy. Hezekiah, king of Judah, faced an armed attack by Assyria, but we shall see God's strong hand of deliverance on the people of Judah. Hezekiah was a godly king who trusted the Lord and who stood against the onslaught of the enemy. Just like Hezekiah, when we choose to believe that God is for us and not against us, and when we choose to "strengthen our feeble hands," He will come and save us. As believers we are assaulted by the enemy in three ways. These assaults threaten to weaken us and destroy our confidence in God. Let us now examine these three assaults symbolized in the confrontation between the Assyrians and God's people.

Lesson Focus
Read Isaiah 35 through 37

I. First Assault: Weak Resources

- Key Passage: Judges 6:14

The first assault that King Sennacherib of Assyria used against the people of God began with the question, "On what are you basing this confidence of yours?" (Isaiah 36:4) This is the question posed to us today as believers as well, and it would be wise for us to evaluate exactly in what or in whom we place our confidence. The field commander serving as spokesperson for King Sennacherib pointed out that they were depending on Egypt, a splintered reed. (Isaiah 36:6) As we learned in the past chapters of Isaiah, Egypt was known for her resources, particularly her massive army and chariots of horses. If the people of Jerusalem had put their confidence in Egypt, they would have failed. But through the strong godly leadership of their king, Hezekiah, they chose to believe that God would deliver them. It is an easy trap for us to fall into when we look at our meager or seemingly weak resources to defend ourselves against the assaults of the enemy, but we must remember like Hezekiah, that He will surely come and save us!!

What stood out to you as you read the Key Box?

_____

_____

_____

Isaiah 26:9

- Applying this Scripture to your life, how does the Lord use the difficult times, times when you feel as though you are under attack, for good?

_____

_____

Isaiah 25:9

- Since one of our best defenses against the assaults of the enemy is to praise the Lord, personalize this passage in Isaiah to fit your personal circumstances of struggle.

_____

_____

Judges 6:11-16

- What did Gideon look at when God asked Him to deliver Israel from the hand of the Midianites?

_____

_____

- What do you consider as your God-given gifts, strengths, and resources and how can you use them and still be dependent on His strength to deliver you?

_____

_____

Genesis 39:19-22

- What gave Joseph the strength to endure prison?

Joshua 1:1-9

- What gave Joshua the strength to be strong and courageous?

The enemy tries to destroy our confidence by having us look at our natural resources, our own strength and abilities. The Scriptures teach us the futility of looking to our own resources to deliver us, but instead instruct us to "trust in the LORD forever, for the LORD, the LORD, is the Rock eternal." (Isaiah 26:4)

II. Second Assault: Temporary, False Peace

- Key Passage: Isaiah 26:3

Any peace that we have apart from God's peace is temporary. God's peace is dependent on trusting in Him alone: "You will keep in perfect peace him whose mind is steadfast, because he trusts in You." The commander of the Assyrian army told the people of Jerusalem not to listen to their king Hezekiah who told them to place their trust in the Lord, "Do not listen to Hezekiah. This is what the king of Assyria says: Make peace with me and come out to me. Then every one of you will eat from his own vine and fig tree (symbols of security and prosperity) and drink water from his own cistern. . ." (Isaiah 36:16) We, too, can be trapped into a "false peace"- a peace that the world offers apart from God. When we feel threatened by an assault, it is easy to seek a solution apart from God. King Hezekiah sent word to Isaiah to pray for the remnant that still survived. We must remember even in the midst of the assaults, to turn to the Lord and cry out to Him to save us.

What stood out to you as you read the Key Box?

_____

_____

_____

<u>John 14:15-27</u>

- What peace does Jesus offer us that is different from the peace that the world offers, and what is His peace based on?

_____

_____

<u>Nehemiah 4:1-6</u>

- Identify the "holes" in your fortification, the weak places where the enemy tries to disrupt God's peace in you and give you a false peace.

_____

_____

III. Third Assault: Misleading Circumstances

- Key Passage: II Chronicles 20:15

The third assault against the people of Jerusalem was to get them to look at the way things appeared. The problem with that is: things are not always as they appear and we need to view them instead through "kingdom perspective." The Assyrian commander threatened, "Do not let Hezekiah mislead you when he says, 'The Lord will deliver us.' Has the god of any nation ever delivered his land from the hand of the king of Assyria?" (Isaiah 36:18) The people were reminded that the Assyrians had already defeated and taken most of the cities in Judah. It certainly appeared that the Assyrians had the upper hand and that Jerusalem was but a "sitting duck" waiting to be captured!! Yet Hezekiah was faithful and the people were silent in the face of the accusations. As people of God, we must not fall into the trap of looking at the circumstantial evidence, but seek the Lord to "strengthen our feeble arms."

What stood out to you as you read the Key Box?

_____

_____

_____

Isaiah 36:18-21

• What merit, if any, is there in remaining silent in the face of your accusers

_____

_____

Isaiah 53:7

• Name the person in Acts who does not open His mouth to defend Himself.

_____

_____

<u>Matthew 14:22-33</u>

• Why did Peter begin to sink when he was walking on the water with Jesus?

_____

_____

• In your life, what circumstances have you looked at that have caused you to sink?

_____

_____

<u>Acts 4:1-4</u>

• Why were Peter and John seized and put in jail?

_____

_____

• Although the Apostles were put into jail and were seemingly defeated, what evidence do we see of victory in this passage?

_____

_____

When Jesus went to the cross, it appeared that He had been defeated, but when we look at the empty tomb, we know that what appeared to be defeat was victory!!

LIFE APPLICATION

➤ Pray for God's perspective when under attack.

➤ When you are struggling with a circumstance that appears hopeless, pray that the Lord will give you "kingdom perspective" to see the situation through His eyes.

➤ Seek peace amidst trials.

➤ Ask the Lord to grant you a greater faith in His strength and power.

PRAYER

A mighty fortress is our God, a Bulwark never failing; our Helper He amid the flood of mortal ills prevailing.

A Mighty Fortress Is Our God
Martin Luther

7 EFFECTIVE PRAYER

The key in this week's lesson is learning to grow in our understanding in the power of prayer. We need to pray all the time not just when things are not going well. Hezekiah was bold to cry out to the Lord in prayer asking Him to extend his life and God answered his prayer. We need to understand that prayer is not just communicating with God, it is working with God. Prayer is most effective when we are bold, when we believe in faith, and when we trust and receive God's promises. Throughout Scripture, Jesus commended men and women of faith.

Meditation
The prayer of a righteous man is powerful and effective. James 5:13-16

Main Theme
As you read the Main Theme, underline words or thoughts most meaningful to you.

In Isaiah 38 and 39, we will consider the value of prayer in our lives. When Hezekiah was thirty-nine years old, he became extremely ill with a life-threatening disease. Isaiah brought him the Word of the Lord which said; "Put your house in order, because you are going to die; you will not recover." (Hezekiah 38:1) Hezekiah responded by praying. We saw in our past lesson that God heard Hezekiah's prayers and the Assyrians were utterly defeated. Now again Hezekiah cries out to the Lord in prayer and God grants him 15 more years to live!! However, when Hezekiah was not being attacked, he neglected to pray in another situation that appeared harmless but would ultimately turn out to be disastrous. The Babylonian king used flattery and trickery to spy on King Hezekiah's storehouses (Isaiah 39:1-8), and eventually the Babylonians conquered Jerusalem, taking for themselves all of the treasures. Hezekiah neglected to pray when asked to open his storehouse, and instead he was led by flattery into a trap. How easy it is for us as well to pray in times of attack, but how equally important it is to remember to pray unceasingly at all times and in all circumstances, seeking the counsel of the Lord.

Lesson Focus
Read Isaiah 38 and 39

I. Bold Prayer

- Key Passage: I Peter 3:12

One of my favorite Scriptures is in Matthew 11:12: "...the kingdom of heaven has been forcefully advancing, and forceful men lay hold of it." One aspect of advancing the kingdom of God is by boldly laying hold of the promises of God through prayer. As believers we are called to be bold in prayer, to use prayer as one of the keys of the kingdom and believe that the gates of hell cannot prevail against it. (Matthew 16:17-19) I used to think of prayer only as something that I was supposed to do to communicate with God, and throughout the years I have learned that prayer is working alongside the Lord to bring His kingdom and His will to earth! What an awesome responsibility we have to advance His kingdom here on earth through prayer. When we pray the Lord's Prayer we often do it by rote, but when we really ponder the words that we are saying, they are powerful indeed: "Thy Kingdom come, thy will be done, on earth as it is in heaven." We must be bold and diligent to go before the Lord in prayer and work towards the advancement of His kingdom here on earth!

What stood out to you as you read the Key Box?

_____

_____

_____

I Peter 3:12, James 5:13-16, and Proverbs 15:29

- To whom is the Lord attentive according to these scriptures?

_____

_____

Hebrews 4:14-16, Hebrews 7:26-28

- What enables us to "approach the throne of grace" confidently and boldly?

_____

_____

Matthew 11:11-12

- How do you think prayer advances the kingdom of God?

_____

_____

We learned from the Scriptures above that God hears the prayers of the righteous and that their prayers are "powerful and effective." We are righteous as believers only because God has given us His righteousness. (II Corinthians 5:21) I am so grateful that I do not have to say the "right" prayers or be perfect to have my prayers answered! Jesus stands as our Advocate, our Intercessor, and our Mediator to plead our case before a holy God. How wonderful that God sees us through His Son Jesus!

II. Believing Prayer

The men and women of the Old Testament prayed and believed that God would hear their cry. Daniel prayed three times a day and believed that God would save him even when thrown in the lions den and in the fiery pit. The psalmist knew that God would answer his prayers: "I waited patiently for the Lord; He turned to me and heard my cry." (Psalm 40) Jesus came to earth and commended those believed that all things are possible with God. Hezekiah turned to prayer when faced with the armed Assyrians. God heard his cry and saved him and the people of Jerusalem. (Isaiah 37:21-35) God not only hears our prayers, He also answers them. It may not be in the way we expected, but He will indeed answer!

What stood out to you as you read the Key Box?

_____

_____

_____

Matthew 21:22-23 and Mark 11:22-25

- What is the common theme in these scriptures, and what do you think is the main block in today's society in our believing so fervently?

_____

_____

Mark 9:17-29

- What was the significant thing that the disciples neglected when trying to heal the young boy whose speech had been robbed?

_____

_____

James 1:6-8

- How do we keep from being double-minded and doubting that God will answer our prayers?

_____

_____

III. Answered Prayer

- Key Passage: 1 John 5:14-15

Years ago, I remember my husband telling me about a patient of his who seemed to have willed himself to die. This man had received a negative, but not life threatening, report but decided to believe the worst. Nehemiah, however, was a man of faith who when told that the walls of Jerusalem were broken down and that Jerusalem and those who had survived the exile were doomed, boldly cried out to God in prayer. In spite of what he had heard, he both believed and received a good report in his heart that his God would not fail him and the people of Jerusalem. King Hezekiah also cried out to God, knowing that God would prevail, and he chose to receive the "good report" before he had evidence to prove it. We, too, must receive God's promises laid forth in His Word and not fall prey to believing the lies of the enemy.

What stood out to you as you read the Key Box?

_____

_____

_____

Isaiah 37:5-11

- What did Isaiah tell the king's officials not to fear?

_____

_____

- If King Hezekiah had listened to the "fearful words" of the Assyrians, what do you think might have happened?

_____

_____

Romans 4:18-21

- Why was Abraham unwavering in his belief and able to receive the promises of God?

_____

_____

- What has been your ongoing prayer that seems like God will never answer?

_____

_____

Mark 11:24

- What is the key element in prayer that enables you to appropriate God's promises?

_____

_____

Isaiah warned the people of Israel that they had forsaken God, had become prayer less, and were serving idols. Although a nation may stray from godly principles, there is always a godly remnant which continues to hold up the standard. For example, Hezekiah reminded his people to turn to God in prayer and to trust Him. Let us be part of that faithful remnant acknowledging the holiness of God and turning to Him in prayer. May we be like Isaiah and say, "Woe to me! I am ruined! For I am a man of unclean lips, and I live among a people of unclean lips, and my eyes have seen the King!" (Isaiah 6:5)

LIFE APPLICATION

> ➤ Be intentional in pursuing a life of prayer.

> ➤ Pray that you will believe and receive God's promises through prayer.

> ➤ Ask God to open your heart and mind through the ministry of the Holy Spirit to the message of the Scriptures.

PRAYER

Open my eyes that I may see wonderful things in your law (Word).

Psalm 119:18

8 COMFORTING GOD'S PEOPLE

This week we enter into the main theme of Isaiah: God's comfort for His people. God comforts us with His Presence by preparing the way, removing obstacles in our lives, and turning darkness into light. In what way do you need to be encouraged? Are you struggling with fear and finding it difficult to trust the Lord? God told the Israelites that He would lead them even along unfamiliar paths (Isaiah 42:16). He will do the same for us!

Meditation

Comfort, comfort, my people, says your God. Speak tenderly to Jerusalem, and proclaim that her hard service has been completed, that her sin has been paid for, that she has received from the Lord's hand double for all her sins. Isaiah 40:1-2

Main Theme

As you read the Main Theme, underline words or thoughts most meaningful to you.

God speaks to the people of Israel through Isaiah to bring them a word of comfort. He calls the people of Israel His "chosen servants," the "redeemed," the ones to whom He will always bring comfort no matter how disobedient or idolatrous they may become. He called them by name and led them back as a tender shepherd leads his flock. What a comfort to us as believers to know that we, too, are the "redeemed," the ones that God leads by His Holy Spirit to return to Him when we sin. The blood of Christ has redeemed us, and He will be with us when we pass through the rivers; they will not sweep over us. (Isaiah 43:1 2) The people of Jerusalem were captured and sent into exile in Babylon. God was with them throughout the ordeal until their "hard service" of exile was completed. He continued to be with them when they returned from exile. Although there are consequences to our sins just as there were consequences for God's chosen people, the Lord will continue to comfort us and tenderly lead us back to Himself. Although He chastens us, He will never forsake us.

Lesson Focus
Read Isaiah 40 through 43

I. Preparing the Way

- Key Passage: Isaiah 40:3-5

> The Jews had a rough road ahead of them as they returned to rebuild Jerusalem and the temple, but the Lord promised to go before them to open the way. The picture we have in Isaiah 40:3 5 is that of repairing roads, removing obstacles, and preparing the way for the coming of a king. The image of a highway is frequently used in Isaiah's prophecy. Ultimately, this word is fulfilled in the ministry of John the Baptist who came to prepare the way for the ministry of Jesus Christ. Isaiah assured the people that although Assyria and Babylon had been instruments of destruction to God's people, they were now gone: "All men are like grass, and all their glory is like the flowers of the field. The grass withers and the flowers fall, because the breath of the Lord blows on them . . . but the Word of our God stands forever." (Isaiah 40:6-8) We, too, can take comfort that God goes before us even in the most difficult of times, preparing the road for our return by removing the obstacles in our lives so that we can draw near to Him.

What stood out to you as you read the Key Box?

_____

_____

_____

Isaiah 40:1-8 and I Peter 1:23-25

- How do the Scriptures help prepare our way in life by showing us how to avoid or remove obstacles?

_____

_____

<u>Matthew 3:1-6</u>

- As John the Baptist prepared the people for Jesus' coming, what did he tell them they must do in order to prepare their hearts for Jesus and His ministry in their personal lives?

_____

_____

II. Turning Darkness into Light

- Key Passage: Matthew 4:16

> God tells the people through Isaiah that He will "lead the blind by ways they have not known, along unfamiliar paths . . ." (Isaiah 42:16) God comforted His people as He lead them out of captivity, guiding them each step of the way. He proclaimed that He would turn darkness into light and make the rough places smooth. Jesus Christ came to be a light to the Gentiles, to those who did not know Him, to a people living in darkness. He brought salvation and eternal life to those who believed. I am so grateful that although I often walk in darkness on an unfamiliar path, I can trust in my Guide, the Light of the world, Jesus Christ. I know the presence of His Holy Spirit in me will show me the way. I need not fear where I am going or if I will know the way. What comfort indeed that gives me as I lean on and trust Him to lead me!

What stood out to you as you read the Key Box?

_____

_____

_____

Psalm 115:1-9 and Isaiah 44:9-11

- According to these scriptures, what causes us to be blind?

_____

_____

- Although those things that occupy most of your time, treasure, and talent may not seem like idols, how can these things take precedence over your seeking the Lord?

_____

_____

Isaiah 42:1-17

- What are God's promises?

_____

_____

- What will happen to those who trust in idols?

_____

_____

- On what "unfamiliar paths" is the Lord leading you, and how is He making the "rough places smooth"?

_____

_____

III. Bringing His Comforting Presence

- Key Passage: Isaiah 49:13

Isaiah told the people that God would bring strength to the weary, increase the power of the weak, and bring streams in the desert. Although the people returning from captivity were weary and discouraged, He promised them that He would give them strength to rebuild their land from a desert into fertile ground again. We, too, often find ourselves in seasons of our lives where we are physically or spiritually dry, feeling as though we are in a desert, discouraged and weary. Isaiah 40 offers us great comfort during these times. The Jewish Rabbis refer to Isaiah 40 as the "Book of Consolation." Isaiah sought to comfort the Jewish remnant in Babylon after their years of captivity and assure them that God was with them and would take them safely home. Today, we, too, can be comforted during our hard times in knowing that God's presence brings us strength and power. (Isaiah 40:31)

What stood out to you as you read the Key Box?

_____

_____

_____

Isaiah 35:3 10

- To whom will God send "streams in the desert," and who will walk on the Way of Holiness?

_____

_____

• Describe what the Lord does for those who hope in the Lord

_____

_____

Isaiah 43:1-21

• Personalize these passages and describe how the Lord will care for you in troubling times.

_____

_____

Isaiah 58:11-12

• What area of your life is like a "sun scorched" land and what can you do to bring God's promise of repair and restoration into your life?

_____

_____

God comforts His people, the ones He created and formed, the ones He redeemed. He promises them that He will prepare the way for them by removing the obstacles. He will turn darkness in their lives to light, and He will bring strength to the weary, and increase the power of the weak. As God's beloved, through believing and receiving His Son Jesus, we will be comforted by His Spirit and experience streams of living water in the dry seasons of our lives.

LIFE APPLICATION

- ➤ Seek His comfort as He leads you in times of repair and restoration.

- ➤ Pray that the Lord will both reveal and remove the obstacles in your way that keep you from drawing near to Him.

- ➤ Trust His guidance as you walk in unfamiliar paths.

PRAYER

Holy Father, Thy wisdom excites my admiration, Thy power fills me with fear, Thy omnipresence turns every spot of earth into holy ground; but how shall I thank Thee enough for Thy mercy which comes down to the lowest part of my need to give me beauty for ashes, the oil of joy for mourning, and for the spirit of heaviness, a garment of praise? I bless and magnify Thy mercy, through Jesus Christ our Lord.

The Knowledge of the Holy
A. W. Tozer

9 GOD'S PURPOSE PREVAILS

One of the challenges we face as Christians is how to remain secure in knowing that God's will is perfect. We "see through a mirror dimly" and it is sometimes difficult to trust the Lord when we are going through difficult times. We must be diligent in worshipping the Lord only and obeying God in all things. As we turn to Him in the "furnace of affliction", He will restore the broken down places in our lives. The key this week is to keep your eyes on the Lord. Practical ways to do that are: prayer, encouraging one another in our faith, meditating on Scripture.

Meditation
From the east I summon a bird of prey; from a far-off land, a man to fulfill my purpose. What I have said, that will I bring about; what I have planned, that will I do. Isaiah 46:11

Main Theme
As you read the Main Theme, underline words or thoughts most meaningful to you.

God's will and His purposes will prevail. Even though Israel was stubborn and rebellious, worshipping wooden idols, and turning from the one true God, the Lord used their affliction to bring them back to Him. The Lord tells the people through Isaiah, "But now listen Israel, whom I have chosen. This is what the Lord says- He who made you, who formed you in the womb, and who will help you; Do not be afraid, O Jacob, my servant... For I will pour water on the thirsty land, and streams on the dry ground; I will pour out my Spirit on your offspring, and my blessing on your descendants." (Isaiah 44:1-3) Although we may turn from the One who created us and will certainly suffer the consequences, the Lord still loves us. He will sustain and rescue us, His beloved children.

Lesson Focus
Read Isaiah 44 through 48.

I. Transformation Through Worship

- Key Passage: Psalm 95:1-6

The people of Israel turned from their Creator choosing to worship other gods. Isaiah 44 describes the idols that the people made: "They know nothing, they understand nothing; their eyes are plastered over so they cannot see, and their minds closed so they cannot understand." (Isaiah 44:18) Although this describes the wooden idols, it also describes the people to whom Isaiah was sent to prophesy. God told Isaiah, "Go and tell this people: 'Be ever hearing, but never understanding; be ever seeing but never perceiving. Make the heart of this people callused; make their ears dull, close their eyes.' " (Isaiah 6:9) The Israelites worshipped wooden false gods, and they as a people took on the same characteristics as the gods they worshipped. I once heard that we become like whomever or whatever we choose to worship. Let us be a remnant transformed through worshipping the Creator God, becoming more like Him as described in Isaiah 11:2, "The Spirit of the Lord will rest on Him- the Spirit of wisdom and of understanding, the Spirit of counsel and of power, the Spirit of knowledge and of the fear of the Lord.

What stood out to you as you read the Key Box?

_____

_____

_____

Romans 12:1-4
How do you think transformation in worship takes place, supplanting our idols?

_____

_____

2 Corinthians 3:18

- Why do you think worship transforms us into Christ likeness?

_____

_____

_____

_____

John 15:19

- What does it mean to be in the world and not of it?

_____

_____

II. The Furnace of Affliction

- Key Passage: Isaiah 48:10

According to the words of Isaiah, God would have given the Israelites peace and protection, if only they had obeyed God: " . . . your peace would have been like a river, your righteousness like the waves of the sea. Your descendants would have been like the sand, your children like its numberless grains; their name would never be cut off nor destroyed from before me."(Isaiah 48:18-19) God's beloved chosen people turned from the Lord, and in His love and mercy for them, He allowed them to suffer the consequences. Yet God proclaims through Isaiah that He will carry them, sustain them, and ultimately rescue them. (Isaiah 46:4) How gracious the Lord is to sustain us as we walk through the "furnace of affliction." (Isaiah 48:10) He promises to "pour out water on (our) thirsty land" because we belong to Him.(Isaiah 44:3-4)

What stood out to you as you read the Key Box?

_____

_____

_____

Isaiah 48:9-11

- Why do you think that the Lord allows us to be "tested in the furnace of affliction"?

_____

_____

Isaiah 30:19-26

Isaiah 48:9-11

- When God's people cry for help what does He do?

_____

_____

Psalm 119:65-72

- What preceded the psalmist's affliction, and why did he say it was good?

_____

_____

Lamentations 3:19-26

- Why are we not abandoned when we go astray?

_____

_____

III. Restoration of Ruins

- Key Passage: Psalm 23:3

God tells the people of Jerusalem through the prophet Isaiah that He will restore Jerusalem. He also promises that Jerusalem will be inhabited once again and the temple will be rebuilt. Throughout Isaiah 44-48, we read the prophecy concerning Cyrus, King of Persia, who will be used as an instrument of the Lord to rebuild the city of Jerusalem. (Isaiah 45:13) The Israelites were stubborn and rebellious, but God sustained them throughout their time of exile in Babylon. He rescued them out of Babylon and rebuilt their ruined city. God's love restores the ruined places in our lives, restoring our worship of Him. He proclaims to us as He did to the Israelites, "I am bringing my righteousness near, it is not far away; and my salvation will not be delayed." (Isaiah 46:13) I am grateful that we can always count on the Lord to restore and rebuild our lives when we give our hearts back to Him.

What stood out to you as you read the Key Box?

_____

_____

_____

Isaiah 44:24-28

- What did the Lord promise to do through King Cyrus of Persia?

_____

_____

- Why do you think that rebuilding the temple was essential to the restoration of Israel?

_____

_____

- What significance does it have that Cyrus, a pagan king, was the one who authorized the rebuilding of the temple?

_____

_____

Nehemiah 2:11-18

- After Nehemiah inspected the damage done to the walls of Jerusalem by the Assyrian army, what does he say will be the result of rebuilding the walls

_____

_____

- What is Nehemiah's reason for being able to undertake the task of rebuilding the walls of Jerusalem?

_____

_____

Daniel 9:1-19

- What does Daniel's prayer reveal as the reasons for the fall of Jerusalem?

_____

_____

- When Daniel prayed for the restoration of God's people in Jerusalem, what assures him that he can make this request to a holy God?

_____

_____

- How does knowing that it is God's great mercy and love that rebuild the broken places in our lives help us to seek restoration and forgiveness?

_____

_____

Amos 9:11-15

- What hope does this passage give you for restoration in your life where your "spiritual walls" have been broken down?

_____

_____

Proverbs 19:20 states, "Many are the plans in a man's heart, but it is the Lord's purpose that prevails." Although the Israelites went their own way, making their own plans and disregarding God, His purpose prevailed as He brought His people back from captivity and poured out streams of water on their dry land. His purposes stand forever and He will always bring us home when we turn to Him and repent.

LIFE APPLICATION

➤ Examine how you spend your time, treasure, and talent to see if your life is truly God-centered.

➤ Ask the Lord to reveal to you what or whom you worship above Him and seek to lay down those things.

➤ Ask the Holy Spirit to inspect the " spiritual walls of your life" that are broken down and pray that the Lord will rebuild those areas.

➤ Turn back to Him and trust that His purposes will prevail, especially in times of affliction.

PRAYER

Our Father in heaven, hallowed be your name, your kingdom come, your will be done on earth as it is in heaven.

Matthew 6:9-10

10 ENGRAVED ON HIS HANDS

Throughout the book of Isaiah, you have come to know God as Sovereign Lord who loves His people even when they stray from Him and draws them back through repentance. At times you may have felt distant from the Lord; perhaps even now you feel this way. This week you will be focusing on Isaiah 40:27-28 describing God's faithfulness to the weary and discouraged. Reflect on the areas in your life where you have been disappointed or are feeling disappointment now and need the Lord's restoration. Isaiah 49:15 says that your name is written on the palms of God's hand. Christ's hands were pierced by nails out of His great love for us.....out of His desire to have our names engraved on His hands forever.

Meditation
See, I have engraved you on the palms of My hands; your walls are ever before Me.
Isaiah 49:16

Main Theme
As you read the Main Theme, underline words or thoughts most meaningful to you.

Isaiah 49 provides a clear picture of the ministry of Jesus. This prophecy was given 725 years before the Lord appeared. Jesus came to reach the disobedient nation of Israel and bring her back to God. Isaiah describes that His ministry would reach far beyond the land of Israel going out to all the nations. Isaiah further describes that God will not forget His promises to Israel and that He has engraved this nation on the palms of His hands. As Christians, we have a right to claim these promises for ourselves because we have been grafted into the seed of Abraham. (Romans 11:11-24) Are you discouraged, perhaps feeling defeated or alone? Look at the wounds on the hands of Jesus and listen to His words, "Behold my hands and feet, and see that it is I." (Luke 24:39) Those wounds on His hands and feet were marks of love and your very name is engraved on the wounds of His hands.

Lesson Focus
Read Isaiah 49

I. The Servant of the Lord

- Key Passage: Philippians 2:6-9

In Isaiah 49:1-7, three applications of these verses seem to fit. Most significantly, the reference is to Jesus Christ, the Servant, sent by God to gather Israel back, to be a light to the Gentiles, and to bring salvation to the ends of the earth. Secondly, we identify Isaiah the prophet, the one whom was sent to gather the nation of Israel back to God, the one who prophesied about the "light to the Gentiles." Thirdly, these verses can be applied to Christians who are called to be like Jesus, having a servant's heart and bringing His light to a dark world. I am always amazed at how Scripture speaks to us in so many ways. Truly, Jesus, the Living Word, is the same yesterday, today, and tomorrow and His Word speaks to every generation. (Hebrews 13:8)

What stood out to you as you read the Key Box?

_____

_____

_____

John 1:1-17

- Who is the Living Word?

_____

_____

- What does the Word accomplish in our lives today?

_____

_____

Ephesians 6:13-17

• Why do you think the Word of God is an essential part of the armor of God, and how does it protect us as a sword protects a warrior?

_____

_____

Isaiah 42:1-7, Isaiah 49:1-7, Isaiah 61:1-3

• Compare these descriptions of the Servant of the Lord (Jesus Christ), and then write a description of the ministry of Jesus.

_____

_____

II. Restoration of Israel

• Key Passage: Isaiah 49:8

The Lord promises in Isaiah 49:8 that He will restore the land of Israel and "reassign its desolate inheritances." He promises to release the captives, those in darkness, and lead them beside springs of water. Throughout the book of Isaiah, we have come to know God as the Sovereign Lord who loves His people through judgment, the consequence of sin, into a place of restoration. What are the "desolate inheritances" in your life--the promises of God that seem empty or desolate in your life? Have you said like Israel, "…My way is hidden from the Lord; my cause is disregarded by my God?" (Isaiah. 40:27) What assurance Isaiah gives that the "Lord is the everlasting God, the Creator of the ends of the earth. He will not grow tired or weary and His understanding no one can fathom." (Isaiah 40: 28) Throughout Isaiah, we have seen God's faithfulness and restoration to His people. He will indeed restore the "desolate places" of our lives as well.

What stood out to you as you read the Key Box?

_____

_____

_____

II Peter 3:8-9

- Since God's promises are our inheritance, what hope do we have concerning the fulfillment of these promises?

_____

_____

Isaiah 49:8-13

- Describe the restoration that God promised Israel.

_____

_____

Isaiah 40:11, 27-31

- What promise do you have for restoration?

_____

_____

III. Engraved on His Hands

- Key Passage: Isaiah 49:16

Isaiah 49:14-16 describes God's love for Israel. Although His beloved people throughout the generations had turned from Him time and time again, He nevertheless engraved their names on His hands, never to forsake them. God saw the "broken down walls of Jerusalem" and provided a way of restoration by sending Nehemiah to head up a team to repair them. (Nehemiah 1) He sees our broken walls ("... your walls are ever before me" Isaiah 49:16), and seeks to restore them through and because of His unquenchable love. The ephod, which the high priest wore, included stones that had the names of the tribes of Israel engraved on them. Jesus, our High Priest, has engraved our name on His hands, ensuring us of His care and love.

What stood out to you as you read the Key Box?

_____

_____

_____

Isaiah 49:14-26

- Why do you think "those who hope in the Lord will not be disappointed"?

_____

_____

- Compare God's love with human love.

_____

_____

Song of Songs 8:6-7

- Describe God's love as written in this passage by inserting the words "God's love" for "love."

_____

_____

- Fill in the following blanks:

   Lord, you have engraved my _____ on the palm of your hand. The walls of my life, some broken down, are ever before you. Bring restoration to me in _____ . Contend with those people and things that contend with me as your Word promises.

LIFE APPLICATION

✙ Pray that the light of Jesus will shine through to the broken places of your life.

✙ Pray for restoration by claiming God's promises to you.

✙ Believe and rejoice that your name is engraved on His hands.

✙ Think about what you would say in a "thank you" note to Jesus.

✙ Ask the Lord to increase your faith and bring you renewed hope in His faithfulness.

PRAYER

Write your blessed name, O Lord, upon my heart, there to remain so engraven that no prosperity, no adversity, shall ever move me from your love.

Thomas a Kempis

11 HEALED BY HIS WOUNDS

This week spend time in recounting the faithfulness of God throughout the Scriptures in your life and the lives of those closest to you. Isaiah 51 offers hope to us just as hope was offered to the people of Israel. The Lord is always looking to make things new. Paul understood the significance of "pressing on" to the goal and looking ahead to God's promise (Philippians 3:12-14). You may be stuck in the past. Remember that Jesus as the "tender shoot" will bring you through needed healing. He paid a great price to bring us freedom so that we could have a hope for the future.

Meditation
But He was pierced for our transgressions, He was crushed for our iniquities; the punishment that brought us peace was upon Him, and by His wounds we are healed. Isaiah 53:5

Main Theme
As you read the Main Theme, underline words or thoughts most meaningful to you.

The wounds Christ bore on the cross heal us both spiritually and physically. It is difficult for me to grasp the love God has for humanity - love that enabled him to sacrifice His only Son on the cross. It is difficult for me to grasp the love of Christ that enabled Him to endure the cross, the love that held Him on the cross. How did He endure the pain, the anguish, and the rejection? It was His love that enabled Him to offer Himself as a sacrifice for our sin. Today we experience His saving, healing power because of the finished work of the cross. When we sing "Amazing Grace," it is our reminder of all Christ suffered as our High Priest that we might be brought into right standing with God and be healed.

Lesson Focus
Read Isaiah 50 through 53

I. Looking Back

- Key Passage: I Chronicles 16:11-12

> Healing takes place when we look back and see the faithfulness of God. Isaiah 51 and 52 give specific steps which believers can take when they feel discouraged and forsaken. God encourages people to look back at the rock from which they were hewn. (Isaiah 51:1-2) Israel was to look back to Abraham and examine his faith. They could see that the Lord was true to His promises to bring forth the nation of Israel from Abraham's seed. When you are discouraged, look back at the way God has worked in your life and those around you. Paul reminded the Corinthian church that they were once adulterers, idolaters, and/or thieves, but now they were washed, sanctified, and justified as believers in Jesus Christ. (I Corinthians 6:9-11) We may not be where we want to be, but when we look back at where we were and see how the Lord has changed us, we have hope. He has changed our hearts and healed our wounds.

What stood out to you as you read the Key Box?

_____

_____

Isaiah 46:9-10

- How is it helpful to us in our spiritual growth to " remember the former things" recall God's hand on our lives?

_____

_____

Isaiah 51:1-3

- What advantage was it to the Israelites to look back to Abraham who gave them birth?

_____

_____

Genesis 19:15-26

- Why do you think the angels told Lot and his family members not to look back as they fled their former sinful city?

_____

_____

- What happened to Lot's wife when she looked back, and how is that a message for us?

_____

_____

Many of the passages in the Bible encourage us to look back at the "former things" for the purpose of seeing how the Lord has transformed us and blessed us. Lot's wife was disobedient and looked back at her old life, struggling to let go of all that she was leaving behind. Let us look back, not desiring our former ways, but rejoicing at how the Lord has delivered us.

II. Looking Ahead

- Key Passage: Philippians 3:12-13

Isaiah 51:4-6 describes that a new day is coming for Israel, God's people. It also looks to the day when the Messiah will come to bring salvation. When we look ahead to the promises of God, we are renewed in spirit and healed by the salvation that the Lord brings. The final verse in this passage promises that God's deliverance will never end. No matter what difficult times we may go through, God is at work delivering us and healing and restoring us! Paul tells us in II Corinthians 4:17, "For our light and momentary troubles are achieving for us an eternal glory that far outweighs them all. So we fix our eyes not on what is seen, but on what is unseen. For what is seen is temporary, but what is unseen is eternal." As we take this eternal perspective, we are able to look ahead, anticipating the future with hope. He has changed our hearts and healed our wounds.

What stood out to you as you read the Key Box?

_____

_____

_____

Isaiah 42:6-9

- What new things was the Lord declaring to His people in the future, and how can we apply these truths to our lives?

_____

_____

Isaiah 51:3-6

- What does the Lord promise to do for Zion in the future, and how do you think that promise encouraged them during times of trials?

_____

_____

- In your times of despair, how does knowing that God will comfort you and have compassion on your brokenness help you to persevere?

_____

_____

II Peter 3:10-14

- What are we called to do while we are waiting on His return?

_____

_____

III. Wounded for Us

- Key Passage: Isaiah 53:6

Isaiah 53 describes Jesus growing up as a tender shoot, marred beyond recognition as He went to the cross, a man of sorrow familiar with suffering. It is a sobering thought to think about the sufferings of Christ. The death that He suffered was what we deserved; yet our sins were laid on Him even though He was sinless. Man was created in God's image, but allowed sin to infiltrate his life. We were separated from God by the sin in our human hearts. *"We all, like sheep, have gone astray." (Isaiah 53:6) "But He was pierced for our transgressions, He was crushed for our iniquities; the punishment that brought us peace was upon Him, and by His wounds we are healed." (Isaiah 53:5)* Sin, our rebellion against God, mortally wounded humanity, bringing about physical and spiritual sickness and death. We ARE forgiven and healed by the completed work on the cross. How grateful I am that Jesus Christ bore our sins, healed our wounds, and set us free!!

What stood out to you as you read the Key Box?

_____

_____

_____

Isaiah 52:13-15; 53:2-12 and 61:1-4

• Using these passages, write a description of Jesus.

_____

_____

I Peter 2:24-25

• Describe how Jesus is able to heal your wounds and bind up your broken heart.

_____

_____

• How does remembering that Jesus carried all of our infirmities and transgressions on the cross enable you to be set free?

_____

_____

Isaiah points out the judgments that God made on His people but also throughout his book, he brings words of comfort that God will redeem His people, He will never forget them, and He is full of compassion. Jesus Christ came to "afflict the comfortable and to comfort the afflicted." Are you comfortable? Are you afflicted? Look to our Great Shepherd and remember that He came to set you free to live in the fullness of His promises. He paid a great price to enable our hearts and our lives to be healed. Love held Him on the cross. While He hung on the cross, our names were engraved on the palms of His hands. The power and completed work of the cross was demonstrated in the resurrection.

LIFE APPLICATION

- ✠ Look back on your life since you received Christ and journal how the Lord has blessed your life.

- ✠ Look forward to the promises in His Word for you.

- ✠ Thank Him for His amazing love that sets you free.

- ✠ Identify an area in your life where you need to receive healing from the Lord.

- ✠ Ask someone to pray with you.

PRAYER

Father, it is a humbling thing to be died for. On this day let me remember that Jesus Christ, your Son, did exactly that for me. And He went to His death knowing full well how often I would forget His love. Let no pride keep me from kneeling at the foot of that cross. In the name of Jesus, my Savior, I pray. Amen.

The Prayers of Peter Marshall

12 THE REDEEMER

The redemptive power of Christ is seen through His love that draws us close to Him. As a believer, you have salvation and redemption through believing and accepting Christ as your Lord and Savior. If you are uncertain that you have accepted Christ as Lord and Savior, take this moment to pray, asking Him to forgive you of your sins and draw you near to Him. The amazing thing is that our Redeemer *every* day continues to redeem our sins, heal our hurts, and help us in our struggles as we turn to Him. God dwells in a humble and contrite heart (Isaiah 66:2) and makes all things new as we submit to Him. We are all in need of daily restoration.

Meditation
For your Maker is your husband - the Lord Almighty is His name - the Holy One of Israel is your Redeemer; He is called the God of all the earth. Isaiah 54:5

Main Theme
As you read the Main Theme, underline words or thoughts most meaningful to you.

As we examine Isaiah 54 through 66, we see the culmination of God's redemption for His people. He promises that His unfailing love and covenant of peace will not be removed, (Isaiah 54:10) and no weapon forged against us will prosper. (Isaiah 54:17) God promises to bring His people out of captivity, to rebuild Jerusalem, and to comfort the contrite (humble). We often find ourselves as believers in a "place of wilderness"—a place where we feel held captive. God's words spoken through the prophet

Isaiah ring true for us today: "Zion will be called new names: Holy People, God Redeemed, Sought-Out, the City-Not-Forsaken." (Isaiah 62:12 Message)

Lesson Focus
Read Isaiah 54 through 66.

I. Drawing Us Back

- Key Passage: Isaiah 54:7

> The Lord speaks to the people of Israel that though they were abandoned for a brief moment, with deep compassion, He will bring them back. (Isaiah 54:7) God judges us and allows us to feel the consequences of our turning away from Him. The people of Israel, God's covenant people, had turned to other gods and had rejected the God of Abraham, Isaac, and Jacob. Throughout the book of Isaiah, we see God's compassion as He reaches down to call His people back to Him. The prophet Isaiah describes how God's brief abandonment of His people felt to them: "…as if you were a wife deserted and distressed in spirit. . ." (Isaiah 54:6) Sometimes, we feel as though God has abandoned us, but He draws us back with cords of love, drawing those who are weary and thirsty back into His life-giving presence. changed us, we have hope. He has changed our hearts and healed our wounds.

What stood out to you as you read the Key Box?

_____

_____

_____

Isaiah 49:14-23

- Although Zion (Israel) thought that the Lord had forsaken her, what does God promise to do to for her sons and daughters?

- How does this promise apply to us as believers and encourage us to respond when God calls us back?

_____

_____

Isaiah 54:1-10

- What does God promise Jerusalem that He will do for her as He calls her back out of captivity?

_____

_____

- In your own experience of desolation and abandonment, how can this scripture be a source of encouragement to you?

_____

_____

Hosea 11:1-4

- How does God call or draw us back to Himself?

_____

_____

God called the Israelites back to Him time and time again. He restored, redeemed, and drew them back with cords of love. I am always amazed at the unending compassion and love God has for His undeserving people!

II. Comforting the Contrite

- Key Passage: Isaiah 57:15

God has promised in His Word that when we humble ourselves and turn to Him, He will hear and restore us.(II Chronicles 7:14) In Isaiah 59:1-2, the people are reminded that the arm of the Lord is not too short to save nor his ear too dull to hear. It is our sins that have separated us from God. (Psalm 66:18) However, when we turn back to Him in humility and true repentance, the Lord, our Redeemer, listens and comforts us. Our children often do things that displease us, but as parents we are quick to comfort them when they recognize their wrong behavior. God is our loving Father who "revives the spirit of the contrite." (Isaiah 57:15)

What stood out to you as you read the Key Box?

Psalm 51:1-17

- How did King David view his sin and what does he claim to be the sacrifice that pleases God?

Isaiah 40:1-5

- How does the Lord comfort His people, and what does it mean to "make the rough ground level"?

_____

_____

Isaiah 57:14-21

- Why do you think that the Lord dwells with the humble, and what does He promise to do in this passage for them?

_____

_____

Isaiah 59:12-21

- What will the Redeemer do for those who humbly repent?

_____

_____

Isaiah 66:1-2

- Whom does the Lord say that He will esteem?

_____

_____

A contrite, humble heart is a resting place for the Lord. The Lord asks in Isaiah 66, "Where is the house you will build for Me?" I pray that we, as the temple of the Holy Spirit, will prepare a place for the Lord by having a humble heart where He can dwell.

II.   Rebuilding Ancient Ruins

- Key Passage: Isaiah 58:12

The Lord promised in Isaiah 58 to satisfy His people in a sun-scorched land and to restore Jerusalem, His holy city. He is the Repairer of Broken Walls and Restorer of Streets with Dwellings. (Isaiah 58:6) God promised to "loose the chains of injustice and set the oppressed free." When the Lord loosens our chains of oppression, He begins a

What stood out to you as you read the Key Box?

_____

_____

_____

<u>Isaiah 58:6-14</u>

- Personalize this passage to fit your circumstances.

_____

_____

- What is our part in the process of God's ongoing restoration of our lives?

_____

_____

<u>Isaiah 60:18-22</u>

- Although Jerusalem had been forsaken, what does the Lord promise to do to restore her?

_____

_____

<u>Isaiah 61:1-4 and Luke 4:16-21</u>

- Describe in your own words Jesus' mission statement as the Redeemer and Repairer of Broken Walls in our lives.

The description of Jerusalem is a picture of complete restoration from a land called "Desolate" to a "crown of splendor in the Lord's hand." (Isaiah 62:1-12)

LIFE APPLICATION

- Allow the Lord to call you back to Him.
- Prepare a place in your heart through prayer and repentance for the Lord to dwell.
- Pray and ask the Lord to bring you restoration from the desolate and broken down places of your life.
- Seek to know the Lord as your Redeemer.

PRAYER

O Lord, You are my Father. I am the clay, You are the potter; I am all the work of Your hand. Do not be angry beyond measure, O Lord; do not remember my sins forever. Oh, look upon us, I pray, for I am all Your people.

Isaiah 64:8-9 (paraphrased)

ABOUT THE AUTHOR

Founder of international nonprofit Drawing Near to God based in Mt. Pleasant, S.C., Joanne Ellison teaches women to make space for God so that God's presence keeps them from being overwhelmed with life.

Driven by a vision to motivate women to pursue a deeper relationship with God, Ellison founded Drawing Near to God in 2000 and has since reached tens of thousands of women through Christian radio and television, blogging, contributions to the Christian Broadcasting Network, social media, her weekly Bible teachings, livestreaming, speaking, books and other resources. She is the author of over 20 Bible study guides, the popular 365-day Bible devotional, *Drawing Near To God*, *Sitting at His Feet* devotional and *Tell Your Heart to Beat Again*.

She is a mother of three, grandmother of 11, great-grandmother of one and has been married for 46 years to Dr. Blount Ellison. Making her home in the Charleston area for most of her life, Ellison is a graduate of the College of Charleston and an active member of Saint Andrew's Church, Mount Pleasant, SC. In her free time, she enjoys spending time with her grandchildren and traveling with her husband.

Ellison is an engaging speaker, writer and Bible teacher. Her speaking style includes both vulnerability and humor and is rooted in her passion for the Bible. She often incorporates stories about her children, grandchildren and travels into her teachings - cycling through Portugal and Copenhagen as well as hiking mountains all over the States have provided many challenges and adventures!

BIBLIOGRAPHY

- Baker, Kenneth, General Editor.. The NIV Study Bible. Grand Rapids, MI: Zondervan Publishing House.
- Benson, Bob, Sr., and Michael W. Benson. Disciplines for the Inner Life. Nashville, TN: Thomas Nelson Publishers. 1989.
- Hayford, Jack, Editor. Spirit Filled Life Bible. Nashville, TN: Thomas Nelson Publisher, 1991.
- Hayford, Jack. Welcoming the Saving Reign of God. Nashville, TN: Thomas Nelson Publisher, 1996.
- Henry, Matthew. Matthew Henry's Commentary. Grand Rapids, MI: Zondervan Publishing House. 1960.
- Job, Ruebin P., and Norman Shawechuch, A Guide to Prayer for Ministers and Other Servants. Nashville: The Upper Room Publisher, 1983.
- McGrath, Alister & J. I. Packer, Editors. Isaiah – John Calvin. Wheaton, IL: Crossway Books, 2000.
- Motyer, Alec. The Prophecy of Isaiah. Downers Grove IL: InterVarsety Press, 1993.
- Peskett, Howard, Isaiah: Trusting God in Troubled Times. Downers Grove, IL: InterVarsity Press, 2001.
- Peterson, Eugene. The Message. Colorado Sprigs, CO:NavPress. 2002
- Stedman, Ray., Adventure through the Bible, Pala Alto: CA: Discovery Publishing. 1997
- Strong, James. Strong's Exhaustive Concordance of the Bible. Nashville, TN:World Bible Publisher, 1986.
- Tozer, A. W. The Knowledge of the Holy. San Francisco: Harpers, 1961.
- Unger, Merril F. The New Ungers Bible Dictionary. Chicago: Moody Press, 1988.
- Vine, W. E., Merril F.Unger, and William White. Vines Expository of Biblical Words. Nashville, TN: Thomas Nelson Publishers. 1985.
- Wiersbe, Warren W. Be Comforted. Colorado Springs, CO:Chariot Victor Publishing, 1992.
- Zodhiates, Spiros. The Hebrew-Greek Key Study Bible. Chattanooga, TN:AMG Publishers, 1984.

www.ingramcontent.com/pod-product-compliance
Lightning Source LLC
Chambersburg PA
CBHW032048040426
42449CB00007B/1024